# VIOLIN SOLOS ON BALKAN FOLK SONGS AND DANCES

## BY COSTEL PUSCOIU
## SOLO VIOLIN PART

**Free audio play along tracks available online!**
*Visit: www.melbay.com/98396*

**Free Piano Accompaniment Parts online!**
*Visit: www.melbay.com/98396*

## MB98396

BILL'S MUSIC SHELF

**Violin Performances by Mihai Puscoiu**

**Sound and Recording by Mihai Puscoiu**

**Accompaniments by Costel Puscoiu**

*Visit us on the Web at www.melbay.com or www.billsmusicshelf.com*

# Contents

# Foreword

It is very difficult to write a (music) book or to talk about Balkan, because the political situation there is very turbulent and radical changes have been made in the last years. The old political frontiers are no more and the new frontiers are changing every day, as in the case of the former Yugoslavia. What will the situation be in 10 years time ? Nobody can answer that. Very possibly a whole new set of frontiers.

The name of the region I am talking about is the Balkan Peninsula which begins at the Balkan Mountains. Geographically this diverse territory stretches from the Adriatic Sea (west) to the Black Sea (east), and from the Carpathian Mountains (north) to the Mediterranean Sea (south). This includes the territories of Bulgaria, Serbia, Croatia, Slovenia, Bosnia, Albania, Macedonia, Greece, European Turkey and Romania (south and east).

The historical developement of the Balkan has always been very turbulent and unpredictable. Politically, the Balkan was a buffer zone between Western Europe and Asia dominated periodically by the Greeks, the Romans, the Byzantines and in the last five centuries by the Ottoman Empire (the turks). The Balkan was, is and shall remain a "cask of dynamite".

Politically the Balkan changes very quickly, but the peoples of this zone do not change. They have remained the same over the last few centuaries. Consider all these determined and courageous peoples, for example the Macedonians, Albanians, Bosnians, Croatians or Serbians: the Ottoman Empire and the former Yugoslavia are no more, but the peoples exist and shall remain here for hunderds of years.

The Balkan is culturally a conglomerate of peoples with very different origins: Thraco-Illiryans (Albanians), Greeks (Greeks), Thraco-Romans (Romanians), Slavs (Bulgarians, Serbians, Croatians, Slovenians, Macedonians) and Ottomans (Bosnians). The languages and alphabets are many and varied: Slavic languages writen in the Cyrillic alphabet (Bulgarian, Macedonian, Serbo-Croatian), Slavic languages writen in the Latin alphabet (Serbo-Croatian, Slovenian), Latin languages (Romanian), Greek language writen in the Greeks alphabet (Greeks).
The religions are also very varied: Eastern Orthodox (Greeks, Bulgarians, Serbians, Romanians, Macedonians), Roman Catholiks (Croatians, Slovenians) and Muslims (Bosnians, Albanians). Ethinic and religious diversity could possibly be one of the explanations for the continuing frictions and the exaggerated nationalism of the Balkan.

This great cultural diversity is also to be felt in the music of these peoples, which forms an important part of their lives and traditions. The types and styles of vocal and instrumental folks music are very different: slow old epic ballads with archaic form and rich ornaments, vital songs with beautiful melodies and various (love, satirical, drinking, lullabies, etc.) texts about all the human feelings, pastoral songs, very dynamic varied, male or female dances for large and small groups danced in open or closed circle, semicircle, straight or winding line.

The difference between the folk music from Macedonia, Romania, Bulgaria, Greece, Serbia, Dalmatia, Turkey or Slovenia is very easy to hear. There are also distinct regional differentiation inside these national styles, with more of less Turkish influence esspecialy to be heard in the slow melodies.

The dances from Balkan are very vital, powerful and metrically varried:
2/4 - Bulgarian horo, Serbian kolo, Romanian hora and sîrba;
3/4 - Slovenian (alpine) dances;
5/8 - Grecian tsakoniko, Romanian rustem;
6/8 - Romanian slow hora, Dalmatian (barcarole) dances;
7/8 or 7/16 - Bulgarian rachenitza, Macedonian dances, Grecian syrto and kalamatiano, Romanian geampara;
9/16 or 9/8 - Bulgarian horo.
The tempos of these dances are often very quick and contain frequent accelerations and decelerations. The rhythm and the meter are often irregular and asymmetric. The famous Hungarian composer and ethno-musicologist, Bela Bartok, was fascinated by the tumultuous rhythms from the Balkan and very often used the term "Bulgarian rhythm" in his books.

The keys and therefore the harmonies used in Balkan music are also different from those of European classical music. They contain more Eastern elements, more chromatics.

The instruments specific to the Balkan area are also varied: violin (gadulka, vioara), lute (lavta, tambura, saz, baglama, cobza), shepherd's flutes (duduk, fluier, kaval, frula), bagpipe (gayda, cimpoi, gora), drum (tapan, defi, tambourine), cymbal (santouri, tambal), shawm (ney, zurna), pan flute (syrinx, nai, muscal), bousouki, guitar, mandolin, accordion, clarinet, contrabass.

VIOLIN SOLOS ON BALKAN FOLK SONGS AND DANCES is only a small, but representative collection of BALKAN MUSIC FOR VIOLIN. The music is pleasant and entertaining, but also useful in enlarging your exotic repertoire. Considerable music pleasure can be found in these wonderful pieces !

**Costel Puscoiu**

## ABOUT THE AUTHOR

Costel Puscoiu was born on August 29, 1951, in Bucharest, Romania. He studied and graduated from the Ciprian Porumbescu College of Music in Bucharest, majoring in Composition and Theory. In Romania he worked as a music teacher, and for some years he was a conductor and researcher at the Institute for Ethnology and Folklore in Bucharest. He was also a member of the Society of Romanian Composers.

His compositions comprise symphonic music (symphonies, cantatas, concertos for viola), chamber music (string quartets, sonatas for clarinet and piano, contemporary pieces for several ensembles, music for pan flute), choir pieces, and film scores. His compositions are often influenced by Romanian folklore and Byzantine liturgies. He has also contributed to several musicological and folkloristic studies and articles.

In September of 1982 Puscoiu moved to the Netherlands from his native Romania; now he is working in the Music School department as a pan flute teacher and a leader of an orchestra at the Free Academy Westvest in Delft. Meanwhile he has become a member of the Dutch Composers Association.

# Rachenitza

Bulgarian

# Angelina

Bulgarian

# Children's Song

Bulgarian

# Quick Circle Dance

Allegro — Bulgarian

# Elena's Horo

Allegro — Bulgarian

# Dajcovo's Horo

Allegro — Bulgarian

# On The Mountain of Zalongou

Moderato — Greek

# Yerakina

9

# Tsakoniko

# My Little Ribbon

# Kalamatiano

# Jasmine

Turk

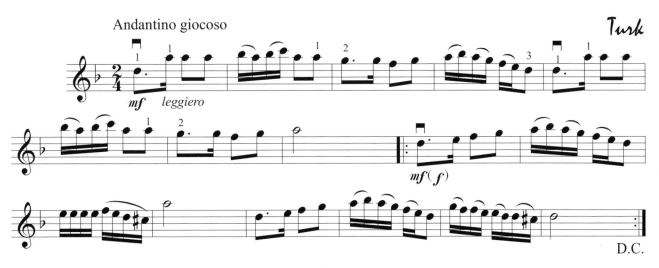

# Dark Blue Grapes

Turk

# My Boy, My Boy

Turk

# Love the Girls

# Radu, Darling

# I'm Going to Cross the River Olt

12

# The Old Man's Dance from Arbore

Romanian

# Good Is the Rosé Wine

Romanian

# Dance from Moldavia

Allegro vivo

Romanian

# Old-fashioned Dance

Andantino cantabile

Romanian

# Sârba from Ploiesti

# Play Again, Your Violin

# There, Behind the Izar

# How Can I Love Somebody ?

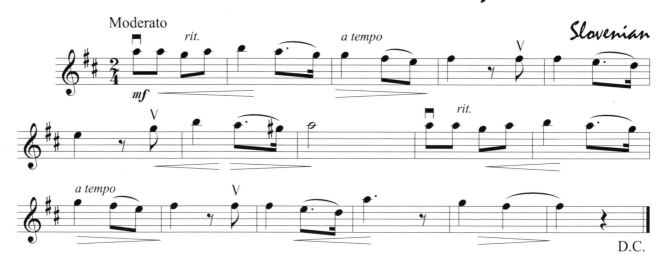

# Dance from Koroska

# The Sun Set Behind the Hill

# Spring

# A Boy and Girl's Desire

# The Stream of Lepenica

# I'll Fall in Sleep

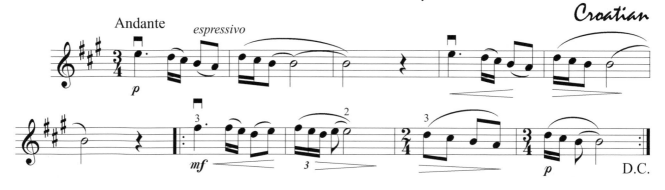

# When the Violets Come Out

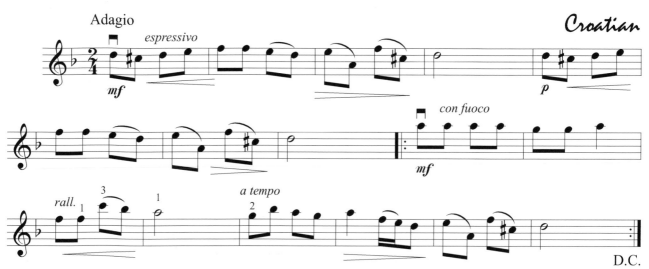

# Marica

Croatian

# Patriotic Song

Croatian

# One Little Marten

Dalmatian

# The Little Shepherdess

Dalmatian

# My Green Rosemary

Moderato

Dalmatian

D.C.

# The Dance of Old Glisha

Allegro vigoroso

Serbian

D.C.

# Miloshevo's Kolo

Allegretto

Serbian

D.C.

# Mara Watch the Sheep

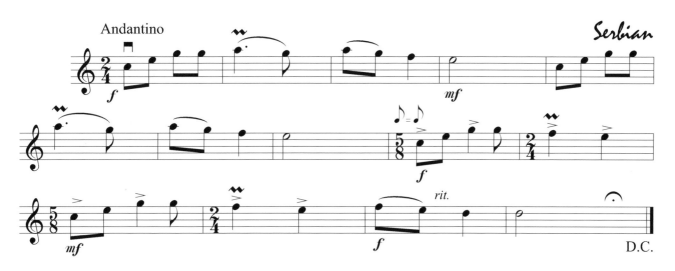

# The Girl from Sumadija

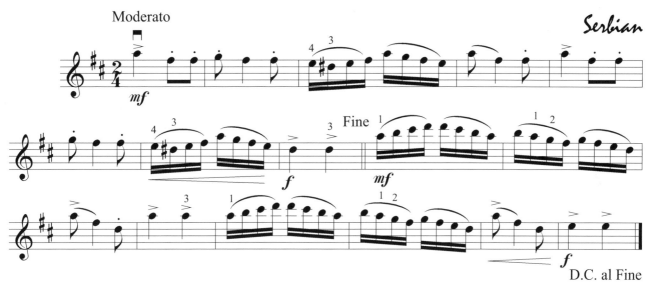

# The Old Women from Gradista

# Vlainjica's Kolo

# When the Roses Bloom

# Sarajevo, Beautiful Place

# Mara Crosses Over the Bosna

Bosnian

D.C.

# The Carnation

Bosnian

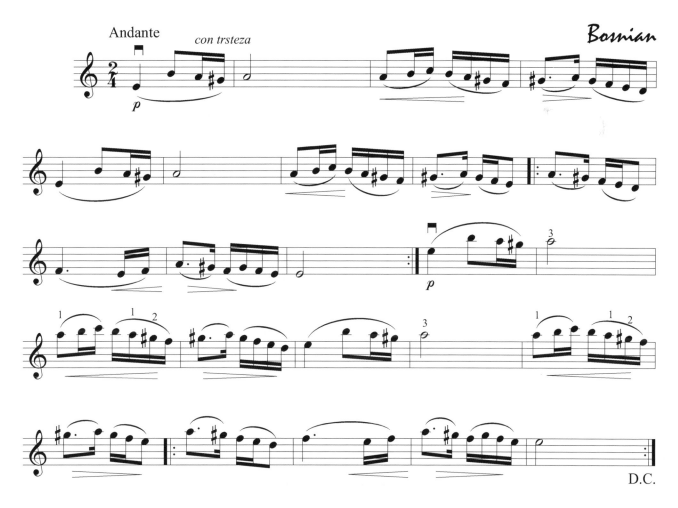

D.C.

# The Big Market from Prijedor

# Jumping Dance

# Coloured Socks

# I Am Marooned in the Mountains

# Who Do You Love?

Andante amoroso

Macedonian

# The First Love

Allegro vivo

Macedonian

# Are You Home My Love?

Allegro vivo

Macedonian

# The Bad Grandfather

Andantino

Macedonian

D.C. al Fine

# Grape Gathering

# I Must Marry a Old Man

# Love Song

# You May not Stay Long in Life, Grey Horse

Andantino

Albanian

# A Room With a Ceiling

Allegretto

Albanian

Made in the USA
Middletown, DE
04 July 2022

68419230R20018